CW00500236

Ninja Foodi Smart Xl Grill Cookbook For The Whole Family

An Effective Guide To Ninja Foodi Smart Xl Indoor Grill And Air Fryer Appliance With Hassle-Free Tasty Recipes To Help You Get Started

Lilla Marcus

Table of Contents

INTRODUCTION 8

CHAPTER 1: SIX METHODS OF NINJA FOODI XL SMART GRILL. 10

GRILL 10

AIR CRISP...10

BAKE 11

ROAST 11

DEHYDRATE 11

THE INSPIRATION BEHIND THIS COOKBOOK 11

WHAT MAKES THE NINJA FOODI SO GREAT? 12

MAKING THE MOST OF YOUR NINJA FOODI......................................12

NINJA FOODI SMART XL GRILL 14

CHAPTER 2: BREAKFAST RECIPES 16

1.   EGGS WITH HAM & VEGGIES 17

2.   EGGS WITH CHICKEN 19

3.   DELICIOUS KALE AND SAUSAGE...21

4.   NINJA FOODI PUMPKIN BREAD..23

5.   DEHYDRATED APRICOT & COCONUT COOKIES..........................25

CHAPTER 3: MEAT RECIPES 28

6.   EASY BEEF SCHNITZEL 29

7.   BEEF WITH PESTO 31

8.   MEDITERRANEAN TENDER PORK ROAST 33

9.   GINGER GARLIC PORK WITH COCONUT SAUCE 35

10.   ALL-TIME PINEAPPLE STEAK 37

11.   AUTHENTIC ASIAN APPLE STEAK..39

12.   CRAZY PINEAPPLE STEAK DRILL...41

CHAPTER 4: FISH RECIPES 44

13. BREADED SHRIMP 45
14. GARLICKY SHRIMP CAESAR SALAD 47

CHAPTER 5: VEGETABLE RECIPES 50

15. CORN PAKODAS 51
16. GARLIC TOMATOES 53
17. TUNA PATTIES 55
18. TUNA AND CUCUMBER SALAD 57
19. ROASTED COD WITH SESAME SEEDS 59

CHAPTER 6: APPETIZERS AND SNACKS RECIPES...............62

20. CRISPY CRAB AND CREAM CHEESE WONTONS.........................63
21. CRISPY POTATO CUBES 65
22. DELIGHTFUL BROCCOLI DISH 66
23. FAJITA SKEWERS..68
24. VEGGIE PITA SANDWICH 70

CHAPTER 7: DESSERTS RECIPES 72

25. GRANOLA MUFFINS..73
26. FEISTY RUM AND PINEAPPLE SUNDAE....................................75
27. LAVA CAKE 77
28. BLUEBERRY SCONES..79
29. ZUCCHINI BREAD..81
30. THE ORIGINAL SICILIAN CAULIFLOWER ROAST 83

CHAPTER 8: MAIN RECIPES 86

31. AIR FRYER BREAKFAST FRITTATA...87

CHAPTER 9: SIDES RECIPES.. 90

32. CRISPY HEALTHY CRABBY PATTIES 91

33. GRILLED CAULIFLOWER AND BROCCOLI...93

CHAPTER 10: POULTRY RECIPES... 96

34. PAPRIKA CHICKEN...97

35. THAI CHICKEN 98

36. TEX MEX CHICKEN 100

37. CREAMY CHICKEN CASSEROLE...102

38. SPICED BREADED CHICKEN 104

39. HEARTY TURKEY BURGER...106

40. SWEET-AND-SOUR DRUMSTICKS...108

CONCLUSION 110

Introduction

N inja Foodi XL Grill Cookbook" introduces you to the Ninja Foodi XL grill and provides you with over 2000 healthy recipes created only for this grill. The book will show you how to prepare a variety of delicious dishes with this versatile grill.

This is the food processor that I have been waiting for since I started cooking. Its large capacity bowl and versatile blade assembly make it an ideal product to use for everyday cooking.

Foodi Smart XL Grill, the latest kitchen appliance by Ninja Foodi, is a food processor that can be used as a griller, slicer, mixer, and blender at homes.

Foodi Smart XL has a large processing bowl of 6.4 quarts capacity that can hold a lot of food for slicing or grilling. The bowl is large enough to make ten servings of coleslaw or salsa, and it is the perfect size for roasting a 3-pound chicken as well.

And the blade assembly can chop, slice shred, mix and blend.

The cookbook starts with an introduction to the Ninja Foodi XL grill. You will learn how to clean the grill, prepare it for use, and then go through the instructions for using this amazing kitchen appliance.

After reading "Ninja Foodi XL Grill Cookbook", you will be ready to make healthy and delicious dishes. You can use this book as a great reference guide for all your grill cooking needs. It can also be a significant learning experience for those who want to get inspired to cook new dishes or gain cooking skills.

When cooking at home, you want a cookbook that delivers. Every cookbook should be tailored to your specific needs, so why not designed for the Ninja Foodi XL Grill? The same team is written by Ninja Foodie XL Grill Cookbook's Ninja Foodie XL Grill Cookbook 1-2-3 series. The Ninja Foodi XL Grill Cookbook offers a practical approach to grilling that will help you get the most from your new grill.

Previous grills have either been too small or not easy to use. I wanted to create the perfect healthy alternative for my family, so I worked on creating a healthier way to cook and grill.

But my mission wasn't only to create a healthy way of cooking but to also make it easy for everyone.

With Ninja Foodi Smart XL Grill everything is easier, and you will be able to enjoy your favorite grilled food with less work and hassle.

While all of our cookbooks provide a great foundation for your grilling adventures, this one is specially designed for this recent addition to the Ninja Foodi XL Grill Cookbook family. We love our Ninja Foodi XL Grill, so we took extra time to make sure we offered the best possible guidance on its proper use.

The Ninja Foodi grill and the other grills differ in several ways. The enormous difference is that the Ninja Foodi Grill heats faster than other grills and cooks much more evenly. This is because the Ninja Foodi Smart XL grill is a solid core-less infrared grill. It uses ceramic infrared burners, which are in a cylinder inside the grill, therefore there are no gaps between the heating elements (unlike most electric grills).

Whether you are a first-time griller or a seasoned pro, The Ninja Foodie XL Grill Cookbook delivers the information you need to ensure that your time spent on the grill will reward and pleasurable.

CHAPTER 1:

Six Methods of Ninja Foodi XL Smart Grill

Now that you have a basic idea of what the Ninja Foodi Smart XL Grill is let's look at the core functions and buttons you should know about. Remember that you have five different cooking types that you can do using your Ninja Foodi Grill.

Grill

At its heart, the Ninja Foodi Smart XL Grill is an indoor grill, so to unlock its full potential, you must understand how the grill function of the appliance works. Let me break it down to you.

Now understand that each set of the Grill is specifically designed for fresh food.

But regardless of which function you choose, the first step for you will always be:

- Place your cooking pot and grill grate in the Ninja Foodi.'
- Let it pre-heat
- Then add your food

The next thing would be to select the Grill function and choose the Grill Temperature. Here you have 4 settings to choose from.

- **Low:** This mode is perfect for bacon and sausages.
- **Medium:** This is perfect for frozen meats or marinated meats.
- **High:** This mode is perfect for steaks, chicken, and burgers.
- **Max:** This is perfect for vegetables, fruits, fresh and frozen seafood, and pizza.

Air Crisp

The Air Crisp mode will help you achieve a very crispy and crunchy golden-brown finish to your food. Using the Air Crisp mode combined with the crisper basket is the perfect combination to cook frozen foods such as french fries, onion rings, and chicken nuggets. Air Crisp is also amazing for Brussels sprouts and other fresh vegetables. Just always shake the crisper basket once or twice to ensure even cooking.

Bake

As mentioned earlier, the Ninja Foodi Smart XL Grill is essentially a mini convection oven. All you need to bake bread, cakes, pies, and other sweet treats is a Cooking Pot and this function. The Pre-heat time for the Bake mode is just 3 minutes.

Roast

The Roast function is used to make everything from slow-roasted pot roast to appetizers to casual sides. Large protein pieces can be put directly in your Ninja Foodi Smart XL Grill and roasted using this function. You can further make this mode more effective by using a Roasting Rack accessory.

Dehydrate

Dehydrators are pretty expensive and take a lot of space in your kitchen. Luckily, you can very easily dehydrate fruits, meats, vegetables, herbs, etc., using just your Ninja Foodi Grill!

The Inspiration Behind This Cookbook

One of my all-time favorite foods is Beef Stew. It's a great meal to batch cook for those busy nights, but it's also what I make for my kids when they're sick. Beef stew is not only hearty and delicious, but it reminds me of my childhood in a way that could bring me to tears. Now, before my Ninja Foodi... Let me tell you how I used to make Beef Stew. First, I would pat dry the beef cubes and season them - this step is a no brainer. Next, I would heat a frying pan on high with some oil and slowly sear the beef, in batches so I didn't overcrowd the pan. It takes a long time and produces a lot of smoke, not to mention, using a lot of oil. Next, I would fill my slow cooker with stock and vegetables. This worked great but took all day to cook and created a lot of dishes to clean.

With the Ninja Foodi, I can sear, simmer, roast, and braise all in one easy-to-clean appliance. The pre-programmed buttons make it so easy, even my kids can make beef stew in it now! This is one of the tabletop appliances on the market that gets hot enough to sear meat properly, so the first thing I made with my Ninja Foodi was beef stew.

What Makes the Ninja Foodi so Great?

Authorization strolls you through how I make beef stew since getting my Ninja Foodi. I open a package of meat, season it, and add it to the Ninja foodi and set it to "sear." In minutes, the temperature has reached 500F so I set a timer after placing the lid on (so there's virtually no smoke at all,) and then come back when the timer has gone off to add the stock and fresh veggies… And voila! In just one hour I have tender, flavorful, juicy, hearty, healthy beef stew!

But it's more than just beef stew! I use my Ninja Foodi for just about everything now, which is why I wanted to create this cookbook (with more than 500 recipes!) to show you how you too can revolutionize the way you cook. You and your family will save time and be healthier in the end - it's really a win-win! (You might also end up feeling like a world-class chef in the end, because everything in this book is so tasty!)

Along with saving money on my energy bill and saving me tons of time around dinner time, this appliance also helped make me and my family healthier! I used to add a lot of oil to the surface of meat before cooking, to prevent it from sticking. I was fed up with losing half a chicken breast on the barbeque so then I started baking them, which didn't offer a lot of flavors. I also used a lot of oil on things like grilled bread, fish, or vegetables. But with the air crisp setting on this machine, you don't need to use any oil whatsoever… which has had an incredible impact on my health. If you're not concerned about oil, this machine will still allow you to enjoy more of the foods that fit into your meal plan – for keto or paleo diets, the Ninja Foodi is a great addition to your kitchen, because of how conveniently you can cook such a variety of proteins.

Making the Most of Your Ninja Foodi

The Ninja Foodi has 6 function buttons which completely replaced my toaster, toaster oven, deep fryer, oven, stovetop, microwave, and even my outdoor barbeque! With this device, I can roast a chicken, a whole fish, or any of my favorite oven meals. I can quickly heat up a piece of pizza or toast. I can air crisp chicken wings or fish sticks for the kids. I can bake a cake or fresh bread. I can dehydrate apple chips or kale chips. I can broil garlic bread or grilled cheese. And probably most impressively… I can grill with no smoke or fire hazards year-round indoors!! Now you try to name an appliance that can do all of that!?!?!

Now you may be wondering – "But is this thing really as good as my barbeque?" The answer is YES and once you try just a few of the recipes from this cook, you will see for yourself. So far, I have grilled everything from shrimp skewers to corn on the cob, to loaded baked potatoes, to hot dogs and yes, even the perfect medium-rare steak. The Ninja Foodi comes with a thermometer probe that is inserted into the center of a seasoned steak, to alert you when it's reached your desire doneness. Once the internal temperature of the steak reaches that temperature, you open the lid and have the perfectly cooked dinner. It really is that easy! Alongside your steak, you can also enjoy perfectly roasted vegetables and potatoes, and you can even enjoy a fresh-baked apple pie for dessert… all from your Ninja Foodi!

One of the finest parts of this machine though is that it reaches a temperature of 500F – this is almost unheard of for a tabletop interior grill. This high temperature allows me to properly sear my food (especially steaks, chicken, or fish) and really allows it to get those tasty grill marks. But this device does more than just sear, as I've told you… because of its unique cyclonic technology, it also circulates the air around your food continuously, which cooks food perfectly, every time.

Ninja Foodi Smart XL Grill

Characteristics	Ninja Foodi AG301 Grill	Ninja Foodi Smart XL Grill
Cooking programs	There are five cook programs. Grill, Air crisp, Bake, Roast, and Dehydrate.	There are six cook programs. Broil, Dehydrate, Air crisp, Roast, Bake, and Grill.
Smart temperature probe	Absent. You have to rely a bit on guesswork to attain that perfect doneness.	Dual sensor Present. To continuously monitor the temperature accuracy for even more perfect doneness. Multi-task away since it cancels the need to watch over the food.
Smart cook system	Absent. Requires frequent checks and guesswork for satisfactory results.	Present. With 4 smart protein settings and 9 customizable doneness levels, all the work is done to input the required setting. Just wait for your food to cook. You could be busy doing your laundry while you cook.
Weight	20 pounds	27.5 pounds
Dimension (L×W×H) inches	12.5 ×16.88×10.59 inches.	18.8 x 17.7 x 14 inches. Therefore, this is the larger option for large-sized family dishes and 50% more grilling space.

CHAPTER 2:

Breakfast Recipes

1. Eggs with Ham & Veggies

Preparation time: 15 minutes

Servings: 10 servings

Ingredients:

- 6 small button mushrooms, quartered

- 6 cherry tomatoes, halved

- 4 shaved ham slices

- 2 tablespoons salad greens

- 1 cup cheddar cheese, shredded

- 2 eggs

- 1 tablespoon fresh rosemary

- Salt and fresh pepper to taste

Directions:

1. In a bowl, add the mushrooms, tomatoes, ham, and greens.

2. Place half of the vegetable mixture in a greased baking pan.

3. Top with half of the cheese.

4. Repeat the layers at once.

5. Make 2 wells in the mixture and carefully crack the eggs in the wells.

6. Sprinkle with rosemary, salt, and black pepper.

7. Put the "Crisper Basket" in the pot of Ninja Foodi Grill.

8. Close the Ninja Foodi Grill with lid in addition select "Air Crisp".

9. Set the temperature to 320 degrees to pre-heat.

10. Press "Start/Stop" to pre-heat.

11. When the display shows "Add Food," open the lid and place the pan into the "Crisper Basket".

12. Close the Ninja Foodi Grill with a lid and set the time for 10 minutes.

13. Press "Start/Stop" to cook.

14. When the cooking time is completed, press "Start/Stop" to stop cooking and open the lid.

15. Cut into equal-sized wedges and serve.

Nutrition:

- Calories: 480 Fat: 30.3 g

- Saturated Fat: 15.1 g Carbohydrates: 20.4 g

- Sugar: 11.3 g Protein: 33.9 g

2. Eggs with Chicken

Preparation time: 10 minutes

Cooking time: 13 minutes

Servings: 2

Ingredients:

- 2 teaspoons unsalted butter, softened

- 2 ounces cooked chicken, chopped

- 4 large eggs, divided Salt and pepper to taste

- 2 tablespoons heavy cream

- 1/8 teaspoon smoked paprika

- 3 tablespoons Parmesan cheese, grated finely

- 2 teaspoons fresh parsley, minced

Directions:

1. Arrange the "Crisper Basket" in the Ninja Foodi Grill.

2. Close the Ninja Foodi Grill with lid also select "Air Crisp".

3. Set the temperature to 320 degrees F to pre-heat.

4. Pick "Start/Stop" to pre-heat.

5. In the bottom of a baking pan, spread butter.

6. Arrange the chicken pieces over the butter.

7. In a bowl, add 1 egg, salt, black pepper, and cream and beat until smooth.

8. Place the egg mixture over the chicken pieces evenly.

9. Carefully crack the remaining eggs on top and sprinkle with paprika, salt, black pepper, cheese, and parsley evenly.

10. When the display shows "Add Food," open the lid and place the pan into the "Crisper Basket".

11. Close the Ninja Foodi Grill with a lid and set the time for 13 minutes.

12. Press "Start/Stop" to cook.

13. When the cooking time is completed, press "Start/Stop" to stop cooking and open the lid.

14. Cut into equal-sized wedges and serve.

Nutrition:

- Calories: 199 Fat: 14.7 g

- Saturated Fat: 6.7 g Carbohydrates: 0.8 g

- Sugar: 0.5 g Protein: 16.1 g

3. Delicious Kale and Sausage

Preparation time: 10 minutes

Cooking time: 10 minutes

Servings: 4

Ingredients:

- 1 medium sweet yellow onion

- 4 medium eggs

- 4 sausage links

- 2 cups kale, chopped

- 1 cup mushrooms

- Olive oil as needed

Directions:

1. Take your Ninja Foodi Smart XL Grill and open the lid, arrange the grill grate, and close the top.

2. Pre-heat Ninja Foodi by demanding the GRILL option and setting it to HIGH and timer to 5 min.

3. Allow it pre-heat till you hear a toot.

4. Add olive oil. Then, arrange sausages over grill grate, lock the lid and cook for 2 minutes, flip sausages and cook for 3 minutes more.

5. Take sausages out.

6. Take a baking pan and spread onion, kale, mushrooms, sausages, and crack eggs on top.

7. Arrange the pan inside the grill and used the BAKE option to bake it at 350°F for 5 minutes.

8. Once done, open the lid and serve.

9. Enjoy!

Nutrition:

- Calories: 236

- Carbohydrates: 17 g.

- Fat: 12 g.

- Protein: 18 g.

4. Ninja Foodi Pumpkin Bread

Preparation time: 10 minutes.

Cooking time: 40 minutes.

Servings: 4

Ingredients:

- 1/3 cup pumpkin puree (canned)

- 3 eggs

- 1/2 cup of vegetable oil

- 1/4 cup water

- 1 cup of sugar

- 1–1/2 cup gluten-free all-purpose flour

- 3/4 teaspoon baking soda

- Salt, pinch 1/3 teaspoon ground cinnamon

- 1/3 teaspoon of nutmeg

- 1 teaspoon pumpkin pie spice

- Powdered sugar for sprinkling

Directions:

- In a prepared mixing bowl, combine eggs, oil, water, and

  pumpkin.

- Use a stand mixer to mix well. Combine the remaining ingredients in a separate noel

- Mix the ingredients of both the bowls

- Once formed the dough, pour it into a loaf pan.

- Place the pan on the wire rack.

- Put the rack inside Ninja Foodi Smart XL.

- Shut the unit and turn on the bake function.

- Set temperate to 325°F for 40 minutes.

- Once done, remove it from the Ninja Foodi Smart and let it get cool.

- Sprinkle with powdered sugar, then serve.

Nutrition:

- Calories: 651

- Fat: 31.5g

- Cholesterol: 123mg

- Carbohydrate: 87.4g

- Dietary fibre: 5.3g

- Protein: 8.9g

5. Dehydrated Apricot & Coconut Cookies

Preparation time: 30 minutes.

Cooking time: 6 hours.

Servings: 24

Ingredients:

- 1 cup semi-dried apricots

- 1 cup coconut, shredded

- 2 cup pitted dates

- 1 cup peanut butter

- 1/4 cup water

- 1/2 teaspoon sea salt (if the butter is unsalted)

Directions:

1. Put the dates and apricot in a grinder and pulse, then add the shredded coconut, peanut butter and salt and pulse again into a thick, coarse mixture.

2. Now start taking out small balls of the mixture with your hands and roll them into balls. Then flatten them using your palms into 1/4 inch thick round cookie shapes.

3. Place the cookie dough on dehydrator sheets. Turn on the Ninja Foodi Smart XL Grill and press the dehydrate button set to dry on high temperature for about 6 hours. Enjoy!

Nutrition:

*   **Calories:** 230

*   **Sodium:** 116mg

*   **Dietary fiber:** 1.6g

*   **Fat:** 17.2g

*   **Carbs:** 5.7g

*   **Protein:** 14.6g

CHAPTER 3:

Meat Recipes

6. Easy Beef Schnitzel

Preparation time: 5 minutes

Cooking time: 12 minutes

Servings: 1

Ingredients:

- ½ cup friendly breadcrumbs

- 2 tablespoons olive oil

- Pepper and salt, to taste

- 1 egg, beaten

- 1 thin beef schnitzel

Directions:

1. Pullout the Crisper Basket and adjust the hood. Choice AIR CRISP fixed the temperature to 350°F (177°C) and set the time to 12 minutes. Select START/STOP to begin preheating.

2. In a shallow dish, combine the breadcrumbs, oil, pepper, and salt.

3. In a second shallow dish, place the beaten egg.

4. Dredge the schnitzel in the egg before rolling it in the breadcrumbs.

5. Put the coated schnitzel in the Crisper Basket. Close the hood and AIR CRISP for 12 minutes. Flip the schnitzel halfway through.

6. Serve immediately.

Nutrition:

- Calories: 520

- Fat: 31 g

- Saturated Fat: 9 g

- Carbohydrates: 38 g

- Fiber: 2 g

- Sodium: 301 mg

Protein: 41 g

7. Beef with Pesto

Preparation time: 10 minutes

Cooking time: 14 minutes

Servings: 4

Ingredients:

- 4 beef (6 oz.) tenderloin steak

- 10 oz. baby spinach, chopped

- 4 cups penne pasta, uncooked

- 4 cups grape tomatoes, halved

- 1/2 cup walnuts, chopped

- 2/3 cup pesto

- 1/2 cup feta cheese, crumbled

- 1/2 tsp. salt

- 1/2 tsp. pepper

Directions:

1. Formulate the pasta as per the instructions on the pack.

2. Drain and rinse, then keep this pasta aside.

3. Season the tenderloin steaks with salt and pepper.

4. Pre-heat Ninja Foodi by demanding the GRILL option and setting it to HIGH for 7 minutes.

5. Once it pre-heat until you hear a beep, open the lid.

6. Place the steaks in the grill grate and cook for 7 minutes.

7. Flip it and cook for 7 minutes.

8. Take a bowl and toss the pasta with spinach, tomatoes, walnuts, and pesto.

9. Garnish with cheese.

10. Serve and enjoy!

Nutrition:

- Calories: 361

- Carbohydrates: 16 g.

- Fat: 5 g.

Protein: 33.3 g.

8. Mediterranean Tender Pork Roast

Preparation time: 10 minutes.

Cooking time: 45 minutes.

Servings: 6

Ingredients:

- 3 pounds pork roasts, cut into 3-inch pieces

- ½ cup Kalamata olives pitted

- ¼ cup fresh lemon juice

- 1 cup beef broth

- 3 tablespoons Cavender's Greek Seasoning to taste

- 1 teaspoon onion powder

- Salt to taste

Directions:

- Put the pork chunks in the inner pot of the Ninja Foodi Smart XL. In a bowl, add Greek seasoning, onion powder, beef broth, lemon juice, olives, and salt to taste. Mix using a spoon and pour the sauce over the pork.

- Close the lid, secure the pressure valve, and select Pressure mode on high pressure for 35 minutes. Press start/stop to start cooking.

- Once the timer is off, open the lid to let out any more steam.

- Use two forks to shred the roast inside to pot and close the crisping lid. Cook on broil mode for 10 minutes, until nice and tender. Serve with a green salad and potatoes or rice.

Nutrition:

- **Energy (calories):** 588

- **Protein:** 61.28g

- **Fat:** 34.18g

- **Carbohydrates:** 4.2g

9. Ginger Garlic Pork with Coconut Sauce

Preparation time: 5 minutes.

Cooking time: 40 minutes.

Servings: 6

Ingredients:

- 3 pounds shoulder roast

- 2 cups of coconut milk

- ½ cup beef broth

- 1 onion, peeled and quartered

- Unchopped parsley leaves for garnish

- 1 tablespoon olive oil

- 3 tablespoons grated ginger

- 1 teaspoon coriander powder

- 1 teaspoon cumin powder

- 3 teaspoons minced garlic

- Salt and black pepper to season

- **Directions:**

- In a bowl, add coriander, salt, pepper, and cumin. Use a spoon to mix them. Season the pork with the spice mixture. Rub the spice onto the meat with your hands. Open the lid of Ninja Foodi Smart XL. Add olive oil, pork, onions, ginger, garlic, broth and coconut milk.

- Close the lid, secure the pressure valve, and select Pressure mode on high for 30 minutes. Press start/stop to start cooking.

- Once the timer has stopped, it performs a quick pressure release. Give it a good stir and close the crisping lid. Cook for 10 minutes on broil mode, until you see a perfect texture and creaminess.

- Dish the meat with the sauce into a serving bowl, garnish it with the parsley and serve with a side of bread or cooked shrimp.

Nutrition:

- Energy (calories): 273

- Protein: 34.28g

- Fat: 10.1g

- Carbohydrates: 9.82g

10.   All-Time Pineapple Steak

Preparation Time: 5-10 minutes

Cooking Time: 8 minutes

Servings: 5

Ingredients:

- ½ medium pineapple, cored and diced

- One jalapeno pepper, seeded and stemmed, diced

- One medium red onion, diced

- Four fillet mignon steak (6-8 ounces)

- 1 tbsp. canola oil

- Salt and pepper to taste

- 1 tbsp. lime juice

- ¼ cup cilantro, chopped

- Chilli powder and ground coriander

Directions:

1. Rub fillets with oil all over the steak and season with salt and pepper

2. Set your Ninja Foodi Smart XL to Grill mode and select High. Adjust the timer to 8 minutes

3. Let it preheat until you hear a beep

4. Arrange fillets over grill grate, cook for 4 minutes

5. Flip and cook for at least 4 minutes more until internal temperature reaches 125 °F

6. Take a bowl and add pineapple, onion, and jalapeno

7. Add lime juice, cilantro, chilli powder, coriander, and mix

8. Serve fillets with pineapple mix and serve

9. Enjoy!

Nutrition:

- Calories: 536

- Fat: 22 g

- Saturated Fat: 7 g

- Carbohydrates: 21 g

- Fibre: 4 g

- Protein: 58 g

11.   Authentic Asian Apple Steak

Preparation Time: 10 minutes

Cooking Time: 15-20 minutes

Servings: 4

Ingredients:

- 3 tbsp. Sesame oil

- 3 tbsp. Brown sugar

- 1 and ½ pounds beef tips

- 4 garlic cloves, minced

- ½ apple, peeled and grated

- 1/3 cup soy sauce

- 1 tsp. ground black pepper

- Salt and pepper to taste

Directions:

1. Take your mixing bowl and add garlic, apple, sesame oil, sugar, soy sauce, pepper and salt

2. Add remaining ingredients and mix well

3. Add beef and coat for 1-2 hours, let it marinate

4. Pre-heat Ninja Foodi Smart XL by pressing the Grill option and set it to "Medium" and timer to 14 minutes

5. Let it pre-heated until it beeps. Arrange beef over grill grate, lock lid and cook until the timer reads 11 minutes

6. After that, cook until the internal temperature reaches 145 ° F, cook for 3 minutes more if needed

7. Serve and enjoy!

Nutrition:

- Calories: 517

- Fat: 29 g

- Saturated Fat: 5 g

- Carbohydrates: 16 g

- Fibre: 4 g

- Protein: 36 g

12. Crazy Pineapple Steak Drill

Preparation Time: 5-10 minutes

Cooking Time: 8 minutes

Servings: 5

Ingredients:

- ½ medium pineapple, cored and diced

- 1 jalapeno pepper, seeded and stemmed, diced

- 1 medium red onion, diced

- 4 fillet mignon steak (6-8 ounces)

- 1 tbsp. canola oil

- Salt and pepper to taste

- 1 tbsp. lime juice

- ¼ cup cilantro, chopped

- Chilli powder and ground coriander

Directions:

1. Rub fillets with oil all over the steak and season with salt and pepper

2. Set your Ninja Foodi to Grill mode and select high, adjust the timer to 8 minutes

3. Let it preheat until you hear a beep

4. Arrange fillets over grill grate, cook for 4m minutes

5. Flip and cook for another 4 minutes more until internal temperature reaches 125 °F

6. Take a bowl and add pineapple, onion, and jalapeno

7. Add lime juice, cilantro, chilli powder, coriander, and mix

8. Serve fillets with pineapple mix and serve. Enjoy!

Nutrition:

- Calories: 536

- Fat: 22 g

- Saturated Fat: 7 g

- Carbohydrates: 21 g

- Fibre: 4 g

- Sodium: 286 mg

- Protein: 58 g

CHAPTER 4:

Fish Recipes

13. Breaded Shrimp

Preparation time: 5 min

Cooking time: 16 min

Servings: 4

Ingredients:

- 2 eggs

- 1-pound shrimp, peeled and deveined

- ½ cup panko breadcrumbs

- 1 teaspoon ginger

- 1 teaspoon garlic powder

- ½ cup onion, peeled and diced

- 1 teaspoon black pepper

Directions:

1. Press the "Air Crisp" button on the Ninja Foodi Smart XL Grill and adjust the time for 16 minutes at 350 degrees F.

2. Combine panko, spices, and onions in one bowl, and whisk eggs in another bowl.

3. Dip the shrimp in the whisked eggs and then dredge in the panko mixture.

4. Place the shrimp in the Ninja Foodi when it shows "Add Food."

5. Grill for about 16 minutes, tossing the patties halfway through.

6. Dish out the fillets in a platter and dish out to serve warm.

Nutrition:

- Calories: 246

- Fat: 7.4 g

- Saturated Fat: 4.6 g

- Carbohydrates: 9.4 g

- Fiber: 2.7 g

- Sodium: 353 mg

- Protein: 37.2 g

14.   Garlicky Shrimp Caesar Salad

Preparation time: 10 minutes

Cooking time: 5 minutes

Servings: 4

Ingredients:

- 1 lb. (454 g) fresh jumbo shrimp

- 1/2 lemon juice

- 3 garlic cloves, minced

- Sea salt to taste

- Freshly ground black pepper to taste

- 2 heads romaine lettuce, chopped

- 3/4 cup caesar dressing

- 1/2 cup Parmesan cheese, grated

Directions:

1. Select START/STOP to preheat.

2. In a large container, throw the shrimp with lemon juice, garlic, salt, and pepper. Let marinate while the grill is warming.

3. After the unit toots to indicate it has preheated, carefully place the shrimp on the Grill Grate. Close the lid and GRILL for 5 minutes.

4. While the shrimp grills, toss the romaine lettuce with the Caesar dressing, then divide evenly among 4 plates or bowls.

5. When cooking is complete, use tongs to remove the shrimp from the grill and place it on top of each salad.

6. Sprinkle with the Parmesan cheese and serve.

Nutrition:

- Calories: 250

- Fat: 8 g.

- Saturated Fat: 3 g.

- Carbohydrates: 22 g.

- Fiber: 3 g.

- Sodium: 370 mg.

- Protein: 36 g.

CHAPTER 5:

Vegetable Recipes

15.   Corn Pakodas

Preparation time: 10 minutes

Cooking time: 8 minutes

Servings: 5

Ingredients:

- 1 cup flour

- ¼ teaspoon baking soda

- ¼ teaspoon salt

- ½ teaspoon curry powder

- ½ teaspoon red chili powder

- ¼ teaspoon turmeric powder

- ¼ cup water

- 10 cobs baby corn, blanched

- Cooking spray

Directions:

1. Insert the Crisper Basket and close the hood. Select AIR CRISP, set the temperature to 425°F (218°C), and set the time to 8 minutes. Select START/STOP to begin preheating.

2. Cover the Crisper Basket with aluminum foil and spritz with the cooking spray.

3. In a bowl, combine all the ingredients, save for the corn. Stir with a whisk until well combined.

4. Coat the corn in the batter and put it inside the basket.

5. Close the hood and AIR CRISP for 8 minutes until a golden-brown color is achieved.

6. Serve hot.

Nutrition:

- Calories: 200

- Fat: 12 g

- Carb: 16 g

- Proteins: 15 g

16.   Garlic Tomatoes

Preparation time: 10 minutes

Cooking time: 15 minutes

Servings: 4

Ingredients:

- 4 garlic cloves, grounded

- 1/4 cup olive oil

- 1 lb. mixed tomatoes

- Salt and black pepper, as desired

- 3 thyme springs, sliced

Directions:

1. Place the cooking pot into the Ninja Foodi Smart XL Grill, then the crisper basket. Ensure the splatter shield is in position and close the lid.

2. Press the AIR CRISP button. Set the temperature to 360°F and set the time for 15 minutes.

3. Press the START/STOP button to preheat the appliance for 3 minutes.

4. Mix the garlic, tomatoes, olive oil, thyme, salt, and black pepper in a bowl.

5. Transfer the coated tomatoes to the crisper basket and close the lid.

Serving suggestions: Serve immediately

Preparation and cooking tips: Shake the basket halfway

Nutrition:

- Calories: 100

- Fat: 0 g.

- Carb: 1 g.

- Proteins: 6 g.

17.   Tuna Patties

Preparation time: 10 minutes

Cooking time: 22 minutes

Servings: 4

Ingredients:

- 2 cans tuna, packed in water

- 1 1/2 tbsp. almond flour

- 1 1/2 tbsp. mayonnaise

- Pinch salt and pepper

- 1/2 tsp. onion powder

- 1 tsp. garlic powder

- 1 tsp. dill, dried

- 1/2 lemon, juiced

Directions:

1. Select the GRILL button on the Ninja Foodi Smart XL Grill and regulate MED settings for 10 minutes.

2. Mingle all the tuna patties ingredients in a bowl and create equal-sized patties from this mixture.

3. Arrange the tuna patties in the Ninja Foodi when it displays ADD FOOD.

4. Grill for about 10 minutes, tossing the patties once in between.

5. Dole out the fillets in a platter and serve warm.

Serving suggestions: Serve with the garlic mayo dip.

Variation tip: You can also use fresh garlic instead of powdered garlic.

Nutrition:

- Calories: 338 Fat: 3.8 g.

- Sat. Fat: 0.7 g.

- Carbohydrates: 8.3 g.

- Fiber: 2.4 g. Sugar 3 g.

- Protein: 15.4 g.

18.   Tuna and Cucumber Salad

Preparation time: 10 minutes

Cooking time: 6 minutes

Servings: 4

Ingredients:

- 2 tbsp. rice wine vinegar

- 1/4 tsp. sea salt, plus additional for seasoning

- 1/2 tsp. pepper, plus additional for seasoning

- 6 tbsp. extra virgin olive oil

- 1 1/2 lbs. (680 g.) ahi tuna, cut into 4 strips

- 2 tbsp. sesame oil

- 1 (10 oz./284 g.) bag baby greens

- 1/2 English cucumber, sliced

Directions:

1. Pull-out the Grill Grate and adjacent the hood. Choice GRILL, fixed the temperature to MAX, and fixed the time to 6 minutes. Select START/STOP to preheat.

2. In the meantime, in a small container, beat together the rice vinegar, 1/4 tsp. of salt, and 1/2 tsp. of pepper. Slowly pour

in the oil while whisking until the vinaigrette is fully combined.

3. Season the tuna with salt and pepper, and drizzle with the sesame oil.

4. As soon as the unit toots to indicate it has preheated, place the tuna strips on the Grill Grate. Close the lid and GRILL for 4–6 minutes. (There is no need to flip during cooking.)

5. While the tuna cooks divide the baby greens and cucumber, slice evenly among 4 plates or bowls.

6. When cooking is complete, top each salad with one tuna strip. Drizzle the vinaigrette over the top and serve immediately.

Nutrition:

- Calories: 250

- Fat: 8 g.

- Saturated Fat: 3 g.

- Carbohydrates: 22 g.

- Fiber: 3 g. Sodium: 370 mg.

- Protein: 36 g.

19.   Roasted Cod with Sesame Seeds

Preparation time: 5 minutes

Cooking time: 7–9 minutes

Servings: 1 fillet

Ingredients:

- 1 tbsp. soy sauce, reduced-sodium

- 2 tsp. honey

- Cooking spray

- 6 oz. (170 g.) fresh cod fillet

- 1 tsp. sesame seeds

Directions:

1. Insert the Crisper Basket and close the lid. Select ROAST, set the temperature to 360°F (182°C), and set the time to 10 minutes. Select START/STOP to preheat.

2. In a small bowl, combine the soy sauce and honey.

3. Spray the Crisper Basket with cooking spray, then place the cod in the basket, brush with the soy mixture, and sprinkle sesame seeds on top.

4. Close the hood and ROAST for 7–9 minutes, or until opaque.

5. Remove the fish and allow to cool on a wire rack for 5 minutes before serving.

Nutrition:

- Calories: 250

- Fat: 8 g.

- Saturated Fat: 3 g.

- Carbohydrates: 22 g.

- Fiber: 3 g.

- Sodium: 370 mg.

- Protein: 36 g.

CHAPTER 6:

Appetizers and Snacks Recipes

20.   Crispy Crab and Cream Cheese Wontons

Preparation time: 10 minutes

Cooking time: 10 minutes per batch

Servings: 6 to 8

Ingredients:

- 24 wonton wrappers, thawed if frozen

- Cooking spray

For the filling:

- 5 ounces (142 g) lump crabmeat, drained and patted dry

- 4 ounces (113 g) cream cheese, at room temperature

- 2 scallions, sliced

- 1½ teaspoons toasted sesame oil

- 1 teaspoon Worcestershire sauce

- Kosher salt and ground black pepper, to taste

Directions:

1. Spritz the Crisper Basket with cooking spray.

2. Insert the Crisper Basket and close the hood. Select AIR CRISP, set the temperature to 350°F (177°C), and set the time to 10 minutes. Select START/STOP to begin preheating.

3. In a medium-size bowl, place all the ingredients for the filling and stir until well mixed. Prepare a small bowl of water alongside.

4. On a clean work surface, lay the wonton wrappers. Scoop 1 teaspoon of the filling in the center of each wrapper. Wet the edges with a touch of water. Fold each wonton wrapper diagonally in half over the filling to form a triangle.

5. Arrange the wontons in the Crisper Basket. Spritz the wontons with cooking spray. Work in batches, 6 to 8 at a time. Close the hood and AIR CRISP for 10 minutes, or until crispy and golden brown. Flip once halfway through.

6. Serve immediately.

Nutrition:

- Calories: 353 Carbs: 11 g

- Fat: 7.5 g Protein: 13.1 g

21.   Crispy Potato Cubes

Preparation time: 10 minutes

Cooking time: 20 minutes **Servings:** 4

Ingredients:

- 1-pound potato, peeled 1 tablespoon olive oil

- 1 teaspoon dried dill 1 teaspoon dried oregano

- 1/4 teaspoon chili flakes

Directions:

1. Pre-heat Ninja Foodi. Press the "AIR CRISP" option and set it to "400 Degrees F" and timer to 20 min.

2. Cut potatoes into cubes.

3. Sprinkle potato cubes with dill, oregano, and chili flakes.

4. Transfer to Foodi Grill and cook for 15 minutes.

5. Stir while cooking, once they are crunchy

6. Serve and enjoy!

Nutrition:

- Calories: 119 Carbs: 20 g

- Fat: 4 g Protein: 12 g

22.   Delightful Broccoli Dish

Preparation time: 10 minutes

Cooking time: 15 minutes

Servings: 4

Ingredients:

- 1/2 tsp. red pepper flakes

- 1/4 cup toasted almonds, sliced

- 1 large broccoli head, cut into florets

- 2 tbsp. extra virgin olive oil

- Pepper and salt to taste

- 2 tbsp. Parmesan, grated

- Lemon wedges

Directions:

1. Take a mixing bowl, add broccoli and toss with olive oil. Season with salt and pepper. Add red pepper flakes and toss well.

2. Pre-heat Ninja Foodi, press the AIR CRISP option, and setting it to 390°F and timer to 15 minutes.

3. Arrange a reversible trivet in the Grill Pan, arrange broccoli crisps in the trivet.

4. Let them roast until the timer runs out.

5. Serve with toasted almonds and enjoy with cheese on top and some lemon wedges!

Nutrition:

- Calories: 181

- Carbohydrates: 9 g.

- Fat: 11 g.

- Protein: 8 g.

23.   Fajita Skewers

Preparation time: 5 minutes

Cooking time: 6 minutes per batch

Servings: 12 Taquitos

Ingredients:

- 1 lb. sirloin steak, cubed

- Olive oil for drizzling

- 1 bunch scallions, cut into large pieces

- 4 large bell pepper, cubed

- 1 pack tortillas, torn

- Salt to taste

- Black pepper, grounded

Directions:

1. Thread the steak, tortillas, scallions, and pepper on the skewers.

2. Drizzle olive oil, salt, black pepper over the skewers.

3. Pre-heat Ninja Foodi by pressing the GRILL option and setting it to MED.

4. Once preheated, open the lid and place 4 skewers on the grill.

5. Cover the lid and grill for 7 minutes.

6. Keep rotating skewers every 2 minutes.

7. Serve warm and enjoy!

Nutrition:

- Calories: 353

- Carbohydrates: 11 g.

- Fat: 7.5 g.

- Protein: 13.1 g.

24.   Veggie Pita Sandwich

Preparation time: 10 minutes.

Cooking time: 9 to 12 minutes.

Servings: 4

Ingredients:

- 1 baby eggplant, peeled and chopped

- 1 red bell pepper, sliced

- ½ cup diced red onion

- ½ cup shredded carrot

- 1 teaspoon olive oil

- ¹/3 cup low-fat Greek yogurt

- ½ teaspoon dried tarragon

- 2 low-sodium whole-wheat pita bread halved crosswise

Directions:

- Preheat Ninja Foodi Smart XL Grill. Select bake, set the temperature to 390°F (199°C) and set the time to 10 minutes. Select START/STOP to begin preheating.

- In the pot, stir together the eggplant, red bell pepper, red onion, carrot, and olive oil. Close the hood and Bake for 7 to

9 minutes, stirring once, until the vegetables are tender. Drain if necessary.

- In a prepared small bowl, thoroughly mix the yogurt and tarragon until well combined.

- Stir the yogurt mixture into the vegetables—stuff one-fourth of this mixture into each pita pocket.

- Place the sandwiches in a baking pan. Place the pan directly in the pot and BAKE for 2 to 3 minutes, or until the bread is toasted.

- Serve immediately.

Nutrition:

- **Energy (calories):** 136

- **Protein:** 6.44g

- **Fat:** 2.79g

- **Carbohydrates:** 23.76g

CHAPTER 7:

Desserts Recipes

25.   Granola Muffins

Preparation time: 10 minutes

Cooking time: 15-20 minutes

Servings: 4

Ingredients:

- 3 ounces plain granola

- 3 handful of cooked vegetables of your choice

- 1/4 cup of coconut milk

- A handful of thyme diced

- 1 tablespoon coriander

- Salt and pepper to taste

Directions:

1. Pre-heat Ninja Foodi. Press the "AIR CRISP" option and set it to "352 Degrees F" and the timer to 20 minutes

2. Take a mixing bowl and add cooked vegetables

3. Take an immersion blender and whiz granola until you have a breadcrumb-like texture

4. Add coconut milk to the granola and add veggies

5. Mix well into muffin/ball shapes

6. Transfer them to pre-heated Ninja Foodi Smart XL Grill and

   cook for 20 minutes

7. Serve and enjoy once done!

Nutrition:

- Calories: 140

- Carbs: 14 g

- Fat: 10 g

Protein: 2 g

26. Feisty Rum and Pineapple Sundae

Preparation time: 10 minutes

Cooking time: 8 minutes

Servings: 4

Ingredients:

- 1/2 cup dark rum

- 1/2 cup packed brown sugar

- 1 tsp. ground cinnamon

- 1 pineapple, cored and sliced

- Vanilla ice cream, for serving

Directions:

1. Take a large-sized bowl and add rum, sugar, cinnamon.

2. Add pineapple slices, arrange them in the layer. Coat mixture, then let them soak for 5 minutes, per side.

3. Pre-heat Ninja Foodi by demanding the GRILL option and situation it to MAX and timer to 8 minutes.

4. Let it pre-heat until you hear a beep.

5. Strain extra rum sauce from pineapple.

6. Transfer prepared fruit in grill grate in a single layer, press down fruit, and lock the lid.

7. Grill for 6–8 minutes without flipping. Work in batches if needed.

8. Once done, remove and top each pineapple ring with a scoop of ice cream, sprinkle cinnamon, and serve.

9. Enjoy!

Nutrition:

- Calories: 240

- Carbohydrates: 43 g.

- Fat: 4 g.

- Protein: 2 g.

27.   Lava Cake

Lava cake is an incredible dessert. It is delightful and mouth-watering.

It can be enjoyed with ice-cream and drinks.

Preparation time: 10 minutes.

Cooking time: 20 minutes.

Servings: 3

Ingredients:

- 4 tablespoons of flour

- 1 egg

- 2 tablespoons of olive oil

- ½ tablespoon of orange zest

- 4 tablespoons of milk

- 1 tablespoon of cocoa powder

- 4 tablespoons of sugar

- ½ tablespoon of baking powder

Directions:

- Place the cooking pot into the Ninja Foodi Smart XL Grill.

- Ensure the splatter shield is in position and close the hood.

- Press the Bake button. Set the temperature up to 320°F and set the time for 20 minutes.

- Press the start/stop button to preheat the appliance for 3 minutes.

- Put together the eggs and sugar in a bowl.

- Add milk, flour, cocoa powder, salt, baking powder, and orange zest to the bowl and stir thoroughly.

- Add the cocoa mix to the ramekins and transfer to the Ninja Foodi Smart XL Grill.

- Close the hood

Serving suggestions: Serve immediately.

Preparation and cooking tips: Grease the ramekins before adding the cocoa mix.

Nutrition:

- Calories: 201kcal

- Fat: 7g

- Carb: 23g

- Proteins: 4g

28.   Blueberry Scones

Blueberry scone is an elegant and sumptuous dessert. It can be enjoyed with wine or orange juice or any fruit drink of your choice.

Preparation time: 10 minutes.

Cooking time: 10 minutes.

Servings: 10

Ingredients:

- 1 cup of white flour

- 2 teaspoons of baking powder

- 1 cup of blueberries

- 2 teaspoon of vanilla extract

- 2 eggs

- ½ cup of heavy cream

- 5 tablespoons of sugar

- ½ cup of butter

Directions:

- Place the cooking pot into the Ninja Foodi Smart XL Grill.

- Ensure the splatter shield is in position and close the hood.

- Press the Bake button. Set the Ninja Foodi smart temperature to 320°F and set the time for 10 minutes.

- Select the start/stop button to preheat the appliance for 3 minutes.

- Mix the flour, baking powder, salt, and blueberries in a bowl.

- In a separate bowl, mix the butter, heavy cream, sugar, vanilla extract, and eggs.

- Mix the two mixtures and then knead until the dough is obtained.

- Form 10 triangles from the dough and arrange them in the cooking pot.

- Close the hood.

Serving suggestions: Serve the scones cold.

Preparation and Cooking Tips: Line the cooking pot with a baking sheet before you arrange the dough.

Nutrition:

- **Calories:** 130 **at:** 2g

- **Carb:** 4g **Proteins:** 3g

29.   Zucchini Bread

Preparation: 15 minutes **Cooking:** 40 minutes **Servings:** 6

Ingredients:

- 2 eggs

- 8 tbsp. (1 stick) unsalted butter, melted

- 1 1/3 cups sugar 1 tsp. vanilla extract

- 1 tsp. ground cinnamon 1/8 tsp. ground nutmeg

- 1/2 tsp. baking soda

- 1/4 tsp. baking powder

- 1/2 tsp. sea salt 1 1/2 cups all-purpose flour

- 1 cup zucchini, grated Nonstick cooking spray

Directions:

1. Close the Crisping Lid. Preheat the unit by selecting BAKE/ROAST, setting the temperature to 325°F, and setting the time to 5 minutes. Select START/STOP to begin.

2. Meanwhile, in a large mixing bowl, combine the eggs, butter, sugar, and vanilla. Add the cinnamon, nutmeg, baking soda, baking powder, and salt and stir to combine. Add the flour, a little at a time, stirring until combined.

3. Wring out the excess water from the zucchini and fold it into the batter.

4. Grease the Loaf Pan or another loaf pan with cooking spray and pour in the batter. Place the pan on the Reversible Rack, making sure the rack is in the lower position. Place the rack in the pot.Close the Crisping Lid. Select BAKE/ROAST, set the temperature to 325°F, and custom the time to 30 minutes or more. Press START/STOP to begin.

5. When cooking is complete, remove the loaf pan from the pot and place it on a cooling rack. Allow the zucchini bread to cool for 30 minutes before slicing and serving.

Tip: Take this recipe for a notch by stirring 1/2 cup of chocolate chips into the batter along with the shredded zucchini in step 3. You can also add walnuts, pecans, or dried cranberries.

Nutrition:

- Calories: 445 Total fat: 17 g.

- Saturated fat: 10 g. Cholesterol: 111 mg.

- Sodium: 734 mg. Carbohydrates: 68 g.

- Fiber: 1 g. Protein: 5 g.

30. The Original Sicilian Cauliflower Roast

Preparation time: 10 minutes

Cooking time: 10 minutes

Servings: 4

Ingredients:

- 1 medium cauliflower head, leaves removed

- ¼ cup olive oil

- 1 teaspoon red pepper, crushed

- ½ cup of water

- 2 tablespoons capers, rinsed and minced

- ½ cup parmesan cheese, grated

- 1 tablespoon fresh parsley, chopped

Directions:

1. Take the Ninja Foodi and start by adding water and place the cook and crisp basket inside the pot. Cut an "X" on the head of cauliflower by using a knife and slice it about halfway down.

2. Take a basket and transfer the cauliflower to it.

3. Then put on the pressure lid and seal it, and set it on low pressure for 3 minutes.

4. Add olive oil, capers, garlic, and crushed red pepper into it and mix them well.

5. Once the cauliflower is cooked, do a quick release, and remove the lid.

6. Pour in the oil and spice mixture on the cauliflower.

7. Spread equally on the surface, then sprinkle some Parmesan cheese from the top.

8. Close the pot with a crisping lid. Set it on Air Crisp mode to 390 degrees F for 10 minutes.

9. Once done, remove the cauliflower flower from the Ninja Foodi transfer it to a serving plate.

10. Cut it up into pieces and transfer them to serving plates. Sprinkle fresh parsley from the top. Serve and enjoy!

Nutrition:

- Calories: 200 Fat: 12 g

- Carb: 16 g Proteins: 15 g

CHAPTER 8:

Main Recipes

31.   Air Fryer Breakfast Frittata

Preparation time: 10 minutes

Cooking time: 20 Minutes

Servings: 1

Ingredients:

- 1/2 pounds of sausage, breakfast sausage

- 3 -5 eggs, beaten

- 1/2 cup Monterey jack cheese

- 4 tablespoons of bell pepper

- 1 green onion

- 1 cayenne pepper to taste

Directions:

1. Mix eggs, sausage, cheese, bell pepper, onion, and cayenne pepper in a large mixing bowl and combine well.

2. Heat the air fryer to 350 degrees for 10 minutes.

3. Spray the basket with oil spray and then pour the mixture inside it.

4. Cook it inside the air fryer for 20 minutes.

5. Once done, serve and enjoy.

Nutrition:

- Calories 1325

% Daily Value*

- Total Fat 95.8 g 123%

- Saturated Fat 35.6 g 178%

- Cholesterol 732 mg 244%

- Sodium 2201 mg 96%

- Total Carbohydrate 38.5 g 14%

- Dietary Fiber 6.8 g 24%

- Total Sugars 25.7 g

- Protein 79.6 g

CHAPTER 9:

Sides Recipes

32. Crispy Healthy Crabby Patties

Preparation time: 5-10 minutes

Cooking time: 10 minutes

Servings: 4

Ingredients:

- Salt and pepper to taste

- 1 egg, beaten

- 1 lemon zest

- 2 tablespoons almond flour

- 2 tablespoons Dijon mustard

- ¼ cup parsley, minced

- 12 ounces lump crabmeat

- ¼ cup mayonnaise, low carb

- 1 shallot, minced

Directions:

1. Yield a mixing bowl and increase all ingredients, mix well, and prepare 4 meat from the mixture.

2. Preheat Ninja Foodi Smart XL by pressing the "AIR CRISP" option and setting it to "375 Degrees F" and timer to 10 min.

3. Let it pre-heat till you hear a toot.

4. Transfer patties to cooking basket and let them cook for 5 minutes, flip and cook for 5 minutes more.

5. Serve and enjoy once done!

Nutrition:

- Calories: 177

- Fat: 13 g

- Sat Fat: 4 g

- Carbohydrates: 2.5 g

- Fiber: 1 g

- Protein: 49 g

33.   Grilled Cauliflower and Broccoli

Preparation time: 10 minutes

Cooking time: 22 minutes

Servings: 4

Ingredients:

- 3 tbsp. olive oil

- 1 head cauliflower, chopped into bite-size pieces

- 1/2 tsp. salt

- 1 large avocado, sliced

- 1/2 cup vegetable broth

- 1/2 cup broccoli sprouts

- 1 tbsp. fresh lemon juice

- 3 garlic cloves, chopped

- 1 lemon zest

Directions:

1. Select the GRILL button on the Ninja Foodi Smart XL Grill and regulate MED settings for 10 minutes.

2. Mingle the cauliflower and broccoli with all other ingredients in a bowl.

3. Arrange the cauliflower and broccoli mixture in the Ninja Foodi when it displays ADD FOOD.

4. Grill for 10 minutes, stirring once in between.

5. Dole out on a plate when grilled completely and serve warm.

Serving suggestions: Serve Grilled Cauliflower and Broccoli over quinoa.

Variation tip: You can also use carrots instead of broccoli.

Nutrition:

- Calories: 226

- Fat: 19.9 g.

- Sat Fat: 3.3 g.

- Carbohydrates: 10.9 g.

- Fiber: 5.8 g.

- Sugar: 2.6 g.

- Protein: 3.5 g.

CHAPTER 10:

Poultry Recipes

34.   Paprika Chicken

Preparation: 5-10 minutes **Cooking:** 30 minutes **Servings:** 4

Ingredients:

- Salt and pepper to taste 1 teaspoon garlic powder

- 1 tablespoon paprika, smoked 2 tablespoons olive oil

- 2 pounds of chicken wings

Directions:

1. Take the chicken wings and coat them with oil

2. Sprinkle with paprika, garlic powder, salt, and pepper

3. Transfer the chicken wings to the Air Crisping basket

4. Set your Ninja Foodi Smart XL to AIR CRISP

5. Cook for 15 minutes per side at 400 degrees F

6. Once done, serve and enjoy!

Nutrition:

- Calories: 792 Fat: 58 g Sat Fat: 15 g

- Carbohydrates: 2 g Fiber: 0 g

- Sugar 58 g

- Protein: 62 g

35.   Thai Chicken

Preparation time: 5–10 minutes

Cooking time 12 minutes

Servings: 3–4

Ingredients:

- 2 lbs. chicken thighs, skinless

- 1 tbsp. olive oil

- 1 cup tomato salsa, fire-roasted

- 1 tsp. fresh ginger, finely grated

- 1/2 cup almond butter

- 1/4 tsp. red pepper flakes, crushed

- 2 tbsp. fresh lime juice

- 1 tbsp. fresh basil, chopped

- 1 tbsp. soy sauce

Directions:

1. Select the GRILL button on the Ninja Foodi Smart XL Grill and regulate the MED settings for 20 minutes.

2. Mingle chicken thighs with salsa, olive oil, almond butter, lime juice, soy sauce, ginger, and red pepper flakes in a bowl and marinate for 3 hours.

3. Arrange the chicken in the Ninja Foodi when it displays ADD FOOD.

4. Grill for about 20 minutes, flipping once in between.

5. Dole out on a platter and serve garnished with fresh basil.

Serving suggestions: Enjoy with sautéed vegetables.

Variation tip: Cashew butter can also be used instead of almond butter.

Nutrition:

- Calories: 323

- Fat: 14.2 g

- Sat. Fat: 3.4 g

- Carbohydrates: 2.1 g

- Fiber: 0.3 g

- Sugar: 0.6 g

- Protein: 44.3 g

36.   Tex Mex Chicken

Preparation time: 5–10 minutes

Cooking time 12 minutes

Servings: 3–4

Ingredients:

- 1 cup tomatoes, chopped finely

- 2 lbs. of chicken breasts

- 1 cup coconut cream

- 1/2 tsp. salt

- 2 tbsp. Mexican seasoning

- 2 tbsp. olive oil

- 1 cup green chilies

Directions:

1. Select the GRILL button on the Ninja Foodi Smart XL Grill and regulate MED settings for 20 minutes.

2. Mingle chicken breasts with all other ingredients in a bowl.

3. Arrange the chicken in the Ninja Foodi when it displays ADD FOOD.

4. Grill for about 20 minutes, flipping once in between.

5. Dole out on a platter and serve warm.

Serving suggestions: Serve the Tex Mex Chicken with grilled bell peppers.

Variation tip: Both fresh and frozen meat can be used for this recipe.

Nutrition:

- Calories: 323

- Fat: 14.2 g.

- Sat. Fat: 3.4 g.

- Carbohydrates: 2.1 g.

- Fiber: 0.3 g.

- Sugar: 0.6 g.

- Protein: 44.3 g.

37.   Creamy Chicken Casserole

Preparation time: 10 minutes.

Cooking time: 45 minutes.**Servings:** 6

Ingredients:

Chicken and mushroom casserole:

- 1/2 pound (1133.98 grams) chicken breasts, cut into strips

- 1/2 teaspoon salt

- 1/4 teaspoon black pepper

- 1 cup all-purpose flour

- 2 tablespoons olive oil

- 1 pound (453.592 grams) white mushrooms, sliced

- 1 medium onion, diced 2 garlic cloves, minced

Sauce:

- 2 tablespoons unsalted butter 2 tablespoons all-purpose flour

- 1 tablespoon lemon juice

- 1 cup half and half cream 1/2 cup Milk

Directions:

- Butter a casserole dish and toss in chicken with mushrooms and all the casserole ingredients.

- Prepare the sauce in a suitable pan. Add butter and melt over moderate heat.

- Stir in flour and whisk well for 2 minutes, then pour in milk, lemon juice, and cream.

- Mix well and pour milk in this sauce over the chicken mix in the casserole dish.

- Press the "power button" of Ninja Foodi Smart XL Grill and turn the dial to select the "bake" mode.

- Press the time button and set the cooking time to 45 minutes.

- Now push the temp button and set the temperature to 350°F.

- Once preheated, place the casserole dish inside and close its lid.

- Serve warm.

Nutrition:

- **Calories:** 409 **Fat:** 50.5g

- **Cholesterol:** 58mg **Carbs:** 9.9g

- **Fibre:** 1.5g

- **Protein:** 29.3g

38. Spiced Breaded Chicken

Preparation Time: 5 minutes

Cooking Time: 11 minutes

Servings: 4

Ingredients:

- ½ pound (227 g) boneless, skinless chicken breasts, horizontally sliced in half, into cutlets
- ½ tbsp. Extra-virgin olive oil
- 1/8 cup bread crumbs
- ¼ tsp. Sea salt
- ¼ tsp. freshly ground black pepper
- ¼ tsp. paprika
- ¼ tsp. garlic powder
- 1/8 tsp. onion powder

Directions:

1. Insert the Crisper Basket of Ninja Foodi Smart and close the hood. Select Air Crisp, set the temperature to 375°F (191°C), and set the time to 11 minutes. Press Start/stop to begin preheating.

2. Brush both sides of the chicken cutlets with the oil.

3. Combine the bread crumbs, salt, pepper, paprika, garlic powder, and onion powder in a Medium shallow bowl. Dredge the chicken cutlets in the bread crumb mixture, turning several times, to ensure the chicken is fully coated.

4. When the Ninja Foodi smart beeps, it has preheated, then place the chicken in the basket. Close the hood and Air Crisp for 9 minutes. Cooking is completed if the internal temperature of the meat reaches at least 165 °F (74 °C) on a food thermometer. If needed, Air Crisp for up to 2 minutes more.

5. Remove the chicken cutlets and serve immediately.

Nutrition:

- Calories: 220

- Protein: 10.85 g

- Fat: 8.07 g

- Carbohydrates: 25.4 g

39. Hearty Turkey Burger

Preparation: 5 minutes **Cooking:** 13 minutes

Servings: 4

Ingredients:

- 1 pound (454 g) ground turkey

- ½ red onion, minced

- 1 jalapeño pepper, seeded, stemmed, and then minced

- 3 tbsp. Bread crumbs 1½ tsp. ground cumin

- 1 tsp. paprika ½ tsp. cayenne pepper

- ½ tsp. sea salt ½ tsp. freshly ground black pepper

- 4 burger buns, for serving

- Lettuce, tomato, and cheese, if desired, for serving

- Ketchup and mustard, if desired, for serving

Directions:

1. Insert the grill grate of Ninja Foodi Smart and close the hood. Select Grill function, set the temperature to High and set the time to 13 minutes. Select Start/stop to begin preheating.

2. In the meantime, in a prepared large bowl, use your hands to combine the ground turkey, red onion, jalapeño pepper, bread

crumbs, cumin, paprika, cayenne pepper, salt, and black pepper. Mix until just combined; be careful not to overwork the burger mixture.

3. Dampen your hands with cool water and form the turkey mixture into four patties.

4. When the Ninja Foodi smart beeps, it has preheated, then place the burgers on the grill grate. Close the hood and grill for 11 minutes.

5. After 11 minutes, check the burgers for doneness. Cooking is completed if the internal temperature reaches at least 165 °F (74 °C) on a food thermometer. If necessary, close the hood and continue grilling for up to 2 minutes more.

6. If the burgers are done, place each patty on a bun. Top with your preferred fixings, such as lettuce, tomato, cheese, ketchup, and/or mustard.

Nutrition:

- Calories: 652 Protein: 25.19 g

- Fat: 51.86 g Carbohydrates: 19.82 g

40.   Sweet-and-Sour Drumsticks

Preparation Time: 5 minutes

Cooking Time: 25 minutes

Servings: 4

Ingredients:

- 6 chicken drumsticks

- 3 tbsp. Lemon juice, divided

- 3 tbsp. Low-sodium soy sauce, divided

- 1 tbsp. peanut oil

- 3 tbsp. Honey

- 3 tbsp. Brown sugar

- 2 tbsp. Ketchup

- ¼ cup pineapple juice

Directions:

1. Insert the Ninja Foodi Basket and close the hood. Select Bake, set the temperature to 350 °F. (177 °C.), and set the time to 18 minutes. Select Start/stop to begin preheating.

2. Sprinkle the drumsticks with 1 tbsp. of lemon juice and 1 tbsp. of soy sauce. Place in the Crisper Basket and drizzle with

the peanut oil. Toss to coat. Close the hood and bake for 18 minutes, or until the chicken is almost done.

3. Meanwhile, in a metal bowl, combine the remaining 2 tbsp. of lemon juice, the remaining 2 tbsp. of soy sauce, honey, brown sugar, ketchup, and pineapple juice.

4. Put the cooked chicken onto the bowl and stir to coat the chicken well with the sauce.

5. Place the metal bowl in the basket. Bake it for about 5 to 7 minutes or until the chicken is glazed and registers 165 °F. (74 °C.) on a meat thermometer. Serve warm.

Nutrition:

- Calories: 442

- Protein: 36.46 g

- Fat: 21.4 g

- Carbohydrates: 25.34 g

Conclusion

With the Ninja Foodie XL Grill Cookbook, you'll learn how to prepare the freshest food any way you like. You'll start with the basics and work your way up to more advanced techniques. With each technique, you'll get step-by-step instructions and helpful hints to make sure your foods turn out just right. Final Ninja Foodie XL Grill Tips:

- If you're new to grilling, start with the basics—the recipes are written for someone with minimal grilling experience.
- If you're a more advanced griller, feel free to use the recipes as a guide and make your own modifications.
- When you're grilling, always keep in mind that safety is the most important thing—if it seems like a recipe may be too complicated or you're not in a position to grill safely, then don't.
- Remember to grill in moderation and always have plenty of water on hand.
- Don't underestimate your Ninja Foodie XL Grill, especially when grilling.
- Have fun and enjoy the summer!

Tired of bland, boring grilled food? The Ninja Foodie XL Grill Cookbook is the perfect way to kickstart your grilling abilities. With great teaching tools like photos with every recipe and a large variety of recipes that range from basic to advanced and everything in between, you'll be well on your way to becoming a ninja griller.

If you own a Ninja Foodie XL Grill Cookbook, then you already know that it's more than just a grill cookbook. You've probably used it in ways that we never imagined. For instance, you may have used it to make "kabobs" by simply placing the meat on a skewer and cooking it on the grill. That's right! You just placed the meat on a skewer and cooked it!

But there's even more to the Ninja Foodie XL Grill Cookbook than this. You can use the cookbook to start your restaurant using your Ninja Foodie XL Grill Cookbook as a menu. You can even make food for customers right in your kitchen and then have them take it back to their homes with their own Ninja Foodie XL Grill Cookbook. This grill is for everyone no matter if he/she is a professional chef or a person who has just started to cook and wants to cook healthy food with no artificial preservatives added. Ninja Foodi Smart XL Grill is easy to use and will help you prepare your favorite recipes in minutes. It will inspire you to try new recipes as well. This grill comes with an excellent customer support service that will answer any question you might have within 24 hours. A smart grill that promises to cook food faster which is safer and healthier, enter the world of technology. From the name itself, Ninja Foodi Smart XL Grill is a grill that is smart and promises convenient for everyone to use. With this grill, it claims to cook meat in a healthy manner by emitting infrared heat from its dome-shaped lid. It sizzles the meat while leaving moisture and then results in a juicy flavor.

You can also use your Ninja Foodie XL Grill Cookbook to barbecue animals such as turkeys, chickens, and ducks on your grill. And you can roast marshmallows on your grill using your Ninja Foodie XL Grill Cookbook. You'll find all the Ninja Foodie XL Grill Cookbook tools that are necessary to do so inside of this cookbook! In conclusion, if you own a Ninja Foodie XL Grill Cookbook, then you'll see that it's more than just a grill cookbook; it's a tool that will allow you to experience many cooking techniques that we could never have imagined!

CPSIA information can be obtained
at www.ICGtesting.com
Printed in the USA
BVHW091433030521
606339BV00006B/869

9 781801 824187